Dandy Dutch Recip

Edited by Mina Baker-Roelofs

Compiled by Mina Baker-Roelofs and Carol Van Klompen
Associate Editors: Miriam Canter, Dorothy Crum, Dianne S
Joan Liffring-Zug Bourret, and John Zug

Cover photographs of Pella, Iowa by Joan Liffring-Zug Bo
Hindeloopen drawings by Sallie Haugen De Reus
Cover design and drawings by Esther Feske
Other designs from: *A Treasury of Art Nouveau Design & Or*

onger is de beste saus.

Hunger is the best sauce.   Dutch Proverb

Ethnic culture and recipes, regional cookbooks, and these popular "Stocking Stuffer" spiral-bound cookbooks are specialties of Penfield Press. For more information please write for a complete catalog.

ISBN 0941016-84-6
Copyright 1991 Penfield Press
www.penfieldbooks.com

Penfield Books
215 Brown Street
Iowa City, Iowa 52245-5801

Table of Contents

About the Editors

Editor Mina Baker-Roelofs is an Associate Professor Emerita of Home Economics at Central College, Pella, Iowa. Mina's career has taken her on many European study tours, including Wageningen, The Netherlands; for personal interest, she has visited Holland twelve times. Born in Holland, Michigan, at what was then Holland Hospital (now the Netherlands Museum), Mina, with husband Harold Roelofs, lives in Pella. As a distinguished home economist, she has nurtured Dutch heritage in many ways, notably serving as editor of the Dutch food section of *Dat is Lekker Kookboek* and as co-editor of *The Pella Collector's Cookbook*.

Contributing Editor Carol Van Klompenburg, author of Penfield books *Delightfully Dutch Recipes and Traditions* and other books, grew up in Orange City, Iowa, and now lives in Pella with her husband and three sons. Carol celebrates a strong Dutch heritage.

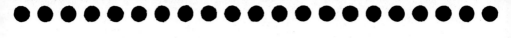

The Artist and Artistry of Hindeloopen

The decorative Hindeloopen designs seen throughout this book are the work of award-winning folk artist Sally Haugen De Reus.

The unique designs, named for the town on the Zuider Zee in the Netherlands, originated with Hindeloopen sailors who were homebound during the winter months. Amateur artists, they painted decorative designs on the wooden parts and furnishings of their home interiors using designs influenced by their travels. Symmetrical floral designs are reminiscent of Norwegian rosemaling, but the motif of birds and borders reflects an influence of travel in the Far East.

Artists can still be found in Hindeloopen carrying on this traditional craft of their ancestors.

A Sampling of Dutch Taste

Dutch Lettuce is the most popular traditional recipe enjoyed by families of Dutch extraction. This preference was drawn from a poll conducted by Mina Baker-Roelofs for a presentation to the Association for the Advancement of Dutch-American Studies. Her survey revealed that, by whatever name, Wilted Lettuce or Dutch "Mess," the leaf lettuce salad, with all its variations, is a number one choice in the Dutch-American household. Mina says that in her family they added boiled potatoes, hard-cooked eggs, a bit of bacon fat, and some bacon bits to the salad. A popular recipe for Dutch Lettuce is included in this book's Salad section.

Second in the poll was Pea Soup, and *Hutspot* (vegetables with chuck or rib roast) was third. Both recipes are in this book: in Soups and Main Dishes.

Appetizers

Buttered Pecan Edam Bowl	8
Cheese Shrimp Bites	9
Cheese Sticks	10
Crab Cocktail	11
Dutch Twists	12
Egg Canapés	13
Eggs Stuffed with Cheese	14
Endive and Eggs	15
Holland Cheese Truffles	14
Party Canapés	16

De Zwaan
Windmill Island
Holland, Michigan

Buttered Pecan Edam Bowl

1 2-pound ball Edam cheese,
at room temperature
1/3 cup beer

2 tablespoons butter, softened
1 teaspoon Worcestershire sauce
dash Tabasco sauce
1/2 cup chopped pecans

Cut a 2- to 3-inch diameter slice from the top of the Edam ball; set slice aside. Do not remove the red wax from cheese. Scoop out the cheese ball, leaving a 1/4-inch shell for the bowl. Shred the cheese and add remaining ingredients. Blend until smooth, adding additional beer (or a little milk) if necessary. Stuff the shell with the cheese mixture and replace the top. Serve at room temperature.

Cheese Shrimp Bites

2 cups shredded Edam or
    Gouda cheese
3 tablespoons flour
1 teaspoon baking powder

1 tablespoon finely minced onion
1/2 teaspoon dill weed
2 eggs, beaten
1/2 cup chopped, cooked shrimp
oil for deep-frying

Combine cheese, flour, baking powder, onion, and dill weed. Add beaten eggs and mix until evenly distributed in the batter, then fold in shrimp. Heat oil to 375° and fry teaspoonfuls of the batter in the hot oil. Fry until golden brown on both sides, about 3 minutes. Drain on absorbent paper. Serve hot. Makes about 36.

Cheese Sticks

The Strawtown Inn, Pella, Iowa

1-1/2 cups grated Gouda cheese,
    divided
1-3/4 sticks butter, softened
1 egg yolk

1/4 teaspoon salt
1 teaspoon Worcestershire sauce
3 cups flour

Combine 3/4 cup of the cheese with the other ingredients. Mix until well blended. Wrap in waxed paper and chill for 2 hours. Roll dough out into a 1/4-inch thickness. Cut into 3x1/4-inch strips. Coat strips with remaining cheese and place on a buttered cookie sheet. Bake at 400° for 15 minutes. Makes 50 to 60 sticks.

Crab Cocktail

Deventer's Yvonne Beerepoot, Dutch home economist, serves this appetizer to American friends.

2 grapefruit, sectioned, chilled	Tabasco sauce to taste
1 6-1/2-ounce can crab meat	black pepper to taste
4 tablespoons mayonnaise	1-1/2 teaspoons dry sherry
3 tablespoons heavy cream	pinch cayenne
1 tablespoon ketchup	1-1/2 teaspoons Worcestershire sauce
	2 tablespoons chopped parsley

Arrange the grapefruit in four fruit cocktail glasses. Divide the crab meat over the fruit. Combine remaining ingredients, except the parsley. Spoon sauce over crab and garnish with parsley.

Dutch Twists

2 cups flour
1 teaspoon salt
2/3 cup chilled shortening
2 tablespoons chilled butter
4 tablespoons water

1 cup shredded Edam or Gouda
    cheese
1 egg white
salt
nutmeg

Sift together flour and salt. Cut in shortening and butter until mixture resembles meal. Gradually add water to form a pie-dough-like mixture. Mix in the cheese. Roll out dough to about 1/4 inch thickness and brush with egg white. Sprinkle with salt and nutmeg, then cut into 5x1/2-inch strips. Twist the strips by holding each end and twisting in opposite directions. Place twists on an ungreased baking sheet, pressing the ends down. Bake at 425° for 10 minutes or until crisp and golden brown. Makes about 3-1/2 dozen.

Egg Canapés

4 slices white bread
3 tablespoons butter, divided
2 tablespoons flour

salt and pepper to taste
4 hard-cooked eggs, chopped
1 cup milk
finely chopped parsley

Cut crusts from bread. Fry bread slices in 2 tablespoons butter until golden and then cut diagonally into triangles; set aside. Add remaining butter to pan; melt, then sprinkle with flour, cooking until bubbly. Add remaining ingredients to make a thick sauce. Place dollops of the sauce on the bread triangles; spread a little of the sauce to the edges. Garnish with parsley. Serves 4.

Eggs Stuffed with Cheese

6 hard-cooked eggs
4 tablespoons butter, melted
2 tablespoons grated Parmesan cheese

1/4 teaspoon salt
1/4 teaspoon pepper
1/2 teaspoon chopped parsley

Halve eggs and remove yolks. Press yolks through a sieve. Add remaining ingredients to yolks; mix well. Fill egg white halves with this mixture and chill.

Holland Cheese Truffles

1/2 cup butter, softened
1 cup shredded Edam or Gouda
    cheese

1/8 teaspoon paprika
1 cup pumpernickel bread crumbs
finely minced parsley

Combine butter, cheese, and paprika. Shape into small balls. Dip half of each ball in pumpernickel crumbs and the other half in parsley. Chill. Makes 24.

Endive and Eggs

12 stalks endive
1/2 teaspoon salt

6 hard-cooked eggs, halved
1/2 cup butter, melted
nutmeg

Separate stalks and wash endive in cold water. Boil endive in salted water for about 15 minutes. Drain and place on a hot platter; garnish with eggs. Sprinkle melted butter with nutmeg and serve with endive. Serves 6.

Party Canapés

Called Bitter Ballen *in Dutch. The word* bitter *comes from "gin and bitter," as these balls are served with Dutch gin or* Jenever.

1 pound chopped veal	3/4 teaspoon nutmeg
3 tablespoons butter	salt and pepper to taste
3 tablespoons flour	rusk crumbs
1 cup milk	1 egg, beaten
1 teaspoon parsley	oil for deep-frying

In a skillet, cook veal until done. In a saucepan, melt butter; sprinkle with flour, stirring until smooth. Remove meat from skillet; add milk to meat drippings, then add this mixture to butter mixture, stirring until smooth. Add meat, parsley, nutmeg, salt, and pepper. Chill. Roll mixture into balls about the size of a walnut. Roll balls in rusk crumbs, then in beaten egg, then in crumbs again. Heat oil to 400° and fry balls in oil until golden. Serve hot with Dijon mustard.

Beverages

Anise Milk	18
Dutch Coffee and Tea	19
Farmer's Son Cocktail	20
Old Dutch Drink	21
Sage Milk	18
Water Chocolate	22

Windmill fireplace
Orange City, Iowa

17

Anise Milk

1 quart milk

1 tablespoon sugar
1 teaspoon anise seeds, crushed

Heat milk just to the boiling point. Add sugar and anise. Serve either hot or cold.

Sage Milk

1 quart milk

1 tablespoon sugar
1 teaspoon ground sage

Heat milk just to the boiling point. Add sugar and sage. Serve hot. Serves 4.

Dutch Coffee and Tea

In the Netherlands, coffee is a stronger brew than in the United States. A product in limited supply, coffee is savored and prepared carefully by the Dutch homemaker. It is usually served in cups smaller than standard cups in the United States, but larger than demitasse cups, and the spoons correspond. For special occasions, coffee is served with real whipped cream that is sweetened and flavored with vanilla.

Tea is the breakfast beverage in many homes in Holland. The "tea cozy" is an essential in the Dutch kitchen. Afternoon tea is a dedicated occasion. Relatives and close friends are known to keep a personal cup at each other's homes. Small cakes and confections are served with the tea, for without these accompaniments, one would have what is called *een naakte tas thee* or "naked" cup of tea.

Farmer's Son Cocktail

Boerenjongens

A special Christmas season drink.

1 pound golden raisins	2 cups brandy
2-1/2 cups water	2 cups sugar
	1 cinnamon stick

Simmer raisins for 10 minutes in water. Add brandy and sugar. Simmer until sugar is dissolved. Cool in a covered bowl, then store in a glass jar with the cinnamon stick for several days. Serve in a stemmed glass with demitasse spoons. **Note:** The Farmer's Daughter Cocktail is similar. Apricots and lemon juice are used instead of raisins and cinnamon. This drink is also served at Christmas or for the birth of a baby.

Old Dutch Drink

After the birth of a baby, whenever friends visit, Kandeel *is served in special glasses or small china cups. Dutch rusk with* mice *(a sprinkled candy topping) is served with this drink.*

1 cinnamon stick	6 egg yolks
10 whole cloves	1/2 cup sugar
1 cup water	2 cups sweet wine

In a saucepan, combine cinnamon, cloves, and water. Simmer for 1 hour. Drain and cool. In the top of a double boiler, beat together yolks and sugar. Add spiced water and wine. Heat mixture; stir constantly until thickened.

Water Chocolate

The Scholte House Museum, Pella, Iowa

Dominie H.P. Scholte, founder of Pella, Iowa, and his wife, Mareah, would enjoy a cup of this water chocolate before retiring. Their lava *(chocolate pot) is on display in the museum.*

2 1-ounce squares sweet chocolate	3/4 cup sugar
1 quart water	1 teaspoon vanilla
1-1/2 teaspoons cornstarch	whipped cream

In a saucepan, melt chocolate carefully. Add water gradually and bring to a boil. Boil for 3 minutes. Blend the cornstarch and sugar with 1/4 cup of the boiling mixture, then stir into the boiling mixture. Boil for 2 to 3 minutes. Add the vanilla and serve hot with whipped cream. Serves 4.

Soups

Carrot Soup	24
Cauliflower Soup	25
Creamy Mushroom Soup	26
Dutch Pea Soup	27
Farmers' Cheese Soup	28
Fish Chowder	29
Vegetable Soup with Meat Balls	30

Old Dutch Mill
Golden Gate Park
San Francisco, California

Carrot Soup

1 large onion, sliced	3-1/2 cups sliced carrots
2 tablespoons butter	1 cup finely chopped celery
1 tablespoon flour	1 teaspoon salt
4 cups beef or chicken broth	1/4 teaspoon pepper

Brown the onion in the butter. Stir in the flour, then add the broth. Heat to a boiling point and cook for 2 minutes. Add remaining ingredients and simmer for 2-1/2 hours. Rub through a sieve and serve hot. Serves 6.

Note: Vegetables may be cooked for a shorter period of time, and the soup puréed in a blender.

Cauliflower Soup

1 small head cauliflower, chopped	1/2 teaspoon salt
3 cups water	1/2 teaspoon pepper
3 cups chicken broth	1-1/4 cups whole milk
4 tablespoons butter	ground nutmeg
4 tablespoons flour	

Cook cauliflower in water until soft.; drain and reserve liquid. Purée in a blender. Combine cauliflower, reserved liquid, and chicken broth. In a large pot, melt butter and stir in the flour until smooth. Add 3 cups of the cauliflower mixture and cook over low heat until hot and smooth. Add the seasonings, milk, and remaining cauliflower mixture. Simmer until hot. Serve garnished with nutmeg. Serves 6.

Creamy Mushroom Soup

2 pounds mushrooms, chopped
1 quart chicken broth
3/4 cup finely chopped onion
3/4 cup diced celery

2 teaspoons fresh chopped basil
5 tablespoons margarine
5 tablespoons flour
1 cup whole milk
salt and pepper to taste

In a large pot, combine mushrooms, broth, onion, celery, and basil. Bring to a boil and reduce heat; simmer for 30 minutes. In a saucepan, melt margarine and stir in flour. Add 2 cups of the broth to the flour mixture and cook until thickened; add to vegetable mixture. Whisk in milk and season to taste. Serves 6.

Dutch Pea Soup

Erwtensoep

2 cups split green peas	salt and pepper to taste
3 quarts cold water	1-1/2 cups celery, chopped
2 pounds pork hocks	3 potatoes, sliced
3 onions, chopped	4 smoked sausages

Wash and soak peas overnight. In a large pot, combine water and peas and boil for 2 hours. Add pork hocks and cook for 1 hour. Add remaining ingredients except the sausages. Cook until smooth and thick, about 3 hours, adding the sausage the last 15 minutes.

Note: The longer the soup simmers the better the taste. The next day the soup tastes even better.

Farmers' Cheese Soup

Boerenkaas Soep

1-1/4 cups finely chopped onion
2 medium-sized potatoes, diced
2 carrots, scraped and cubed
1-1/2 cups cauliflower flowerets
1/2 cup chopped celery
4 to 5 tablespoons margarine

4 to 5 cups chicken broth
4 slices bacon
4 slices thickly cut bread,
   homemade is best
4 thick slices of Gouda cheese

Sauté vegetables in margarine for 5 minutes. Add broth and bring to a boil. Reduce heat and simmer for 20 to 25 minutes or until vegetables are tender. In a skillet, fry bacon until crisp. Drain. Fry bread in bacon grease until browned on both sides; drain. Pour soup into a casserole and float bacon slices on top. Cover each slice with a slice of bread and cheese. Broil for 2 to 3 minutes or until cheese melts. Serves 4.

Fish Chowder

2 slices lean bacon, chopped
1 onion, diced
2 cups vegetable or fish stock
2 cups diced potatoes
1 teaspoon salt
1/4 teaspoon pepper

1 pound white fish, chopped
2 tablespoons butter
2 tablespoons flour
3 cups milk, divided
6 soda crackers

In a saucepan, fry bacon and onion until browned. Add stock, potatoes, seasonings, and fish. Cook until potatoes are soft. In another pan, melt butter and stir in flour. When smooth, add 2 cups milk. Stir and cook until thickened, then add to stock mixture. Crumble crackers and add to stock mixture with remaining milk. Bring to a boil and serve hot. Serves 6.

Vegetable Soup with Meat Balls

Using tiny meat balls as a source of flavor for soup is common practice in Holland.

salt and pepper to taste
3/4 pound ground beef
1-1/2 quarts boiling water
1 large onion, finely chopped

1/2 cup uncooked rice
vegetables, chopped
   (carrots, celery, any variety,
   but fresh if possible)

Salt and pepper ground beef to taste and shape into firm balls about the size of a small egg. Place balls in a soup kettle; pour boiling water over them. (Water must be boiling to prevent meat balls from breaking.) Reduce the heat and simmer meat for 10 minutes. Add the onion, rice, and other vegetables. Add more water if a thinner soup is desired. Bring to a boil again, then reduce to simmer and continue to cook until rice and vegetables are tender, about 20 minutes.

Salads

Dutch Chef Salad	32
Dutch Coleslaw	33
Dutch Lettuce	34
Dutch Potato Salad	35
Ham Pudding	36
Herring Salad	37
Hussar Salad	38

Klokkenspel (glockenspiel)
Pella, Iowa

Dutch Chef Salad

1 head leaf lettuce, torn into
    bite-sized pieces
1 6-1/2-ounce can tuna, drained
1 cucumber, peeled and thinly sliced
1 cup cubed Edam or Gouda cheese

2 medium-sized tomatoes, cut in
    wedges
1 cup thinly sliced radishes
French dressing

Arrange lettuce at both ends of an oblong salad bowl or platter. Arrange the tuna, cucumber, cheese, tomatoes, and radishes in rows. Serve with French dressing. Serves 4 to 6.

Dutch Coleslaw

7 to 8 cups shredded cabbage
1/2 cup minced onion
1/2 cup chopped pimiento
1/2 cup sour cream
1/2 cup minced celery
3 tablespoons chopped green pepper
salt and pepper to taste
Dressing:
1 teaspoon dry mustard

1 tablespoon sugar
1/2 teaspoon salt
2 tablespoons flour
1/4 teaspoon paprika
1/2 cup cold water
1 egg
1/4 cup vinegar
2 tablespoons butter

Combine ingredients and toss to coat. Moisten with dressing and toss again.
Dressing: Combine mustard, sugar, salt, flour, paprika, and water. In the top of a double boiler beat egg and add water mixture. Heat over boiling water until thick, then blend in vinegar and butter. Pour over salad preferably while warm.

Dutch Lettuce

1 tablespoon butter or margarine
1 tablespoon flour
1/2 plus 1/3 cup water, divided
2 egg yolks (or 1 whole egg)
1/2 cup sugar

1/2 plus 1/3 cup vinegar, divided
1 head leaf lettuce
1 tablespoon chopped onion
4 hard-cooked eggs, sliced
6 strips bacon

Melt butter and stir in flour. Add 1/2 cup water and bring to a boil while stirring. Beat egg yolks and add sugar and 1/2 cup vinegar. Blend into the hot mixture. Bring to a boil. Combine the lettuce, onion, and hard-cooked eggs. Cut bacon into small pieces and fry until browned; remove and drain on absorbent paper. Add 4 tablespoons of the hot mixture to the skillet with the remaining water and vinegar; bring to a boil. Toss the bacon with the lettuce mixture, then pour the contents of the skillet over the lettuce mixture; toss to coat. Serves 6.

Dutch Potato Salad

3-1/2 pounds cooked potatoes, diced
4 hard-cooked eggs

1/2 head lettuce, shredded
1/2 pound crisp-fried bacon, crumbled
1/3 cup chopped onion

Dressing:
3 tablespoons flour
2 tablespoons sugar
1/4 teaspoon salt
1/8 teaspoon paprika

2 eggs, beaten
3/4 cup water
3/4 cup vinegar
1/2 cup sour cream
1 teaspoon prepared mustard

Combine all salad ingredients and toss with dressing.

Dressing: In a saucepan, combine flour, sugar, and seasonings. Add eggs and water; cook over low heat until thickened. Add vinegar and blend well. Fold in sour cream and mustard. Pour over salad and toss to coat. Serves 12 to 15.

Ham Pudding

1 envelope unflavored gelatin	1 pound boiled ham, chopped
2 cups hot bouillon	4 sweet pickles, chopped
1/2 teaspoon salt	2 hard-cooked eggs, sliced
1/2 teaspoon pepper	mayonnaise to taste

Dissolve gelatin in hot bouillon; add salt and pepper. Cool until thickened. Fold in ham and pickles. Pour into six individual molds and chill until firm. Unmold and garnish with egg slices and mayonnaise.

Herring Salad

2 salted herrings, filleted
1 cup cubed pickled beets
1 cup cubed tart apples
1-1/2 cups cubed boiled potatoes

1/2 cup cubed pickled gherkin
2 hard-cooked eggs, chopped
1/2 cup chopped pickled onion
1 cup mayonnaise
salt and pepper to taste

Soak fish fillets in cold water overnight. Drain fish and cut into small pieces. Mix well with beets, apples, potatoes, pickles, eggs, and onions. Season mayonnaise and add to fish mixture; mix together. Chill before serving. Serves 6 to 8.

Hussar Salad

A famous Dutch dish for fall and winter.

1/2 pound cooked beef, diced
2 tart apples, chopped
2 pickled beets, chopped
1/2 cup diced bread-and-butter pickles
6 medium-sized cooked potatoes,
    diced
2 tablespoons diced pickled onion
1 small yellow onion, chopped
2 tablespoons oil

2 tablespoons vinegar
1 tablespoon prepared mustard
salt and pepper to taste

Garnishes:
lettuce
mayonnaise
2 hard-cooked eggs, sliced
1 tomato, cut into wedges

Mix meat, apples, beets, pickles, potatoes, and the onions. Combine remaining ingredients; pour over salad mixture and marinate overnight. Serve over lettuce; garnish with mayonnaise, eggs, and tomato wedges. Serves 8 to 10.

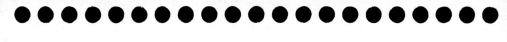

Breads, Sandwiches, and Pancakes

Currant Bread
Krentenbrood

This bread is often a gift at Easter time.

1/2 cup shortening
1/2 cup sugar
1-1/2 tablespoons salt
3 cups scalded milk
1 cup brown sugar

2 eggs, beaten
3 cups currants
1 teaspoon nutmeg
1-1/2 teaspoons cinnamon
1 package active dry yeast
10 cups flour

In a large bowl, combine shortening, sugar, and salt. Scald milk and add to shortening mixture. Cool to lukewarm and add sugar, eggs, currants, spices, and yeast. Gradually beat in the flour, then knead for 10 minutes. Cover and let rise until doubled. Punch dough down and let rise again until doubled. Divide into seven loaves and place in lightly greased 8-1/2x4-1/2x2-1/2-inch loaf pans. Bake at 300° for 45 minutes. **Note:** You may want to divide 1 loaf into small buns.

Dutch Honey Bread

1 cup honey
1 cup brown sugar
6 drops of anise flavoring
1 teaspoon crushed anise seed
3 cups flour

1 tablespoon butter, softened
1/2 cup cold water
1/2 cup milk
1-1/2 teaspoons baking soda
2 teaspoons hot water

Mix honey and sugar. Add anise flavoring and seeds. Add flour alternately with butter, water, and milk. Dissolve soda in hot water, add to dough, and blend well. Pour into two greased 9x5x3-inch loaf pans and bake at 350° for 50 to 60 minutes or until done.

Note: Instead of anise flavorings, 2 teaspoons cinnamon, 1/3 teaspoon ground cloves, and 1/3 teaspoon nutmeg can be substituted.

Dutch Onion Rye Bread

2 packages active dry yeast	1 teaspoon salt
1 cup lukewarm water	2-1/2 cups rye flour
2 cups milk, scalded	1 envelope onion soup mix
1/4 cup dark molasses	5 cups sifted all-purpose flour
1/4 cup oil	1 egg white, slightly beaten

Soften yeast in water. Combine milk, molasses, oil, and salt; cool to lukewarm. Stir in the rye flour. Add yeast mixture and soup mix. Add enough of the white flour to make a stiff dough. Knead for 10 minutes. Place dough in a greased bowl and turn to coat. Cover and let rise until doubled, about 1 hour. Divide dough into three portions and roll each out to a 12x12-inch square. Roll each square up tightly and seal well. Place loaves seam side down on a greased baking sheet. With a sharp knife, gash tops diagonally every 2-1/2 inches; brush with egg white. Cover and let rise for 45 minutes. Bake at 375° for 20 minutes or until light brown. Brush with egg white; bake for 15 to 20 minutes longer. Cool on racks.

Dutch Rye Bread

2 cups rye grits*
1 cup white flour
1/2 cup brown sugar
1 teaspoon salt

2 cups buttermilk
1-1/2 teaspoons baking soda
2 tablespoons dark molasses
2 tablespoons vegetable oil

Mix the first four ingredients in a large mixing bowl. In a smaller bowl, mix buttermilk and baking soda. Add molasses and oil. Add this mixture to the first bowl and mix well, but do not beat. Pour into a greased bread pan and set aside for 1/2 hour. Bake at 350° for 1 hour. Remove from oven and invert another bread pan over the loaf. Remove from pan when cold.

*Rye grits are available in most health-food stores.

Note: Wrap with waxed paper and store in refrigerator.

Dutch Sugar Bread

Ralph Jaarsma, Jaarsma Bakery, Pella, Iowa
This is an old family recipe from the Province of Friesland.

1 package active dry yeast
1/2 cup lukewarm water
2 cups milk, scalded
2 tablespoons sugar
2 teaspoons salt

1 teaspoon cinnamon
1 tablespoon shortening
6-1/2 to 7 cups sifted flour, divided
1/2 pound sugar cubes, chopped
(optional)

Soften yeast in water. Combine hot milk, sugar, salt, cinnamon, and shortening. Cool to lukewarm; stir in 2 cups flour and add the yeast mixture. Add remaining flour, enough to make a stiff dough. Knead 10 minutes. Place in greased bowl and turn to coat. Cover and let rise for 1-1/2 hours or until doubled. Punch dough down and let rise again until doubled, about 45 minutes. Fold sugar cubes into dough and let rest for 10 minutes. Divide into two lightly greased 9x5x3-inch loaf pans. Let rise until doubled, about 1 hour. Bake at 400° for 50 minutes.

Graham Bread

1 package active dry yeast	2 tablespoons molasses
3 to 3-1/2 cups white flour, divided	3 tablespoons shortening
1-3/4 cups milk	1-1/2 teaspoons salt
1/4 cup brown sugar	2 cups graham flour

Combine yeast with 2 cups of the white flour. Scald milk and add sugar, molasses, shortening, and salt. When cooled add to yeast mixture. Beat with an electric mixer for 3 to 4 minutes. Stir in the graham flour and enough of the white flour to make a moderately stiff dough. Knead 8 to 10 minutes. Place dough into a greased bowl and turn to coat. Cover and let rise until doubled. Punch dough down and divide in half. Let rest 10 minutes. Shape into two loaves and place into two lightly greased 9x5x3-inch loaf pans. Cover and let rise until doubled. Bake at 375° for 40 to 45 minutes. Cool on wire rack.

Orange Peel Bread

1 cup molasses
1 cup sugar
1 egg, beaten
5 cups flour

1 teaspoon baking powder
1 cup cold coffee
2 teaspoons baking soda
1 cup candied orange peel

In a large bowl, combine molasses, sugar, and egg. Sift together flour and baking powder. Dissolve baking soda in coffee. Add the flour mixture and coffee mixture alternately to the molasses mixture. Fold in orange peel. Pour into a greased and floured 9x5x3-inch loaf pan and bake at 350° for 1-1/2 hours or until done. Slice thin to serve.

Candied Orange Peel

rind of 2 oranges, finely cut
2 cups water, divided

1/2 cup molasses
1/2 cup sugar

Cook rind in 1 cup water for a few minutes. Drain and add remaining ingredients; cook until liquid boils down. Spread on rack to dry.

Holland Cheese Supper Sandwiches
Royal Netherlands Embassy, Washington, D.C.

4 tablespoons butter, softened and
    divided
2 teaspoons prepared mustard
6 1/2-inch-thick slices trimmed
    white bread

1 pound sliced Edam or Gouda cheese
1/2 cup milk
1 egg
1/4 teaspoon salt
1/8 teaspoon pepper

Blend 2 tablespoons of the butter and mustard; spread on the trimmed slices of bread. Divide the cheese and layer on three slices of bread; cover with remaining bread. Combine the milk, egg, and seasonings. Dip the sandwiches into the milk mixture. Fry sandwiches in remaining butter until golden on both sides. Serves 3.

Meat and Egg Open-Faced Sandwich

Uitsmijter is a dish for people in a hurry who want to eat something substantial. It is a favorite luncheon dish in Holland, frequently ordered in the "fast food," small restaurants.

butter or margarine	2 eggs
2 slices of white bread	dill pickles
4 thin slices boiled ham or roast beef	mustard

Butter the bread and cover with the meat slices. Fry the eggs in small amount of the butter. (Do not over cook yolk of egg.) Put fried egg on top of meat slices; garnish with the pickles. Serve with the mustard and salt and pepper. Serves 1.

Apple Pancakes
Appel Pannekoeken

2 medium-sized tart apples
2 cups flour
1/2 teaspoon salt

4 large eggs
2 cups milk
12 tablespoons butter, melted
sorghum or syrup

Peel, quarter, and core apples. Cut into 1/4-inch slices. Combine flour and salt. Make a well in the flour mixture and pour the eggs into the well. Gradually mix the eggs into the flour. Gradually add milk and beat until just smooth. In an 8- to 9-inch skillet, melt 2 tablespoons butter. Add 1/4 of the apple slices and cook until lightly browned. Pour 1 cup of the batter over the apple slices and cook for 2 to 3 minutes or until browned around the edges. Invert the pancake and cook the other side until browned. Roll the pancake and cover with foil to keep warm. Fry the remaining pancakes the same way. Serve hot with sorghum and remaining butter. Serves 4.

Big Dutch Pancakes

1/4 cup sugar
2-1/2 cups flour
2 teaspoons baking powder
1 teaspoon salt
1 teaspoon baking soda

2 eggs, beaten
3 cups buttermilk
1/4 cup butter, melted
oil for frying
1-1/2 cups raisins, divided
molasses and brown sugar, topping

Sift together dry ingredients; make a well in the center. Combine egg, buttermilk, and butter. Pour egg mixture into the well and beat until smooth. In skillet, heat oil until hot and add enough batter to cover bottom. Cook until bubbles form on the top of pancake; sprinkle with raisins. Turn and cook the other side. Keep warm while cooking remaining pancakes. Serve with molasses and brown sugar if desired. **Note:** Precooked sausages can be placed in the center.

Rice Pancakes

2 eggs, separated
1/3 cup sugar
cinnamon to taste

1/2 cup flour
2-1/2 cups cold cooked rice
butter
sugar for topping

Beat egg yolks with sugar and cinnamon. Beat egg whites until stiff. Fold flour, rice, and egg whites into yolk mixture, in that order. Fry tablespoonfuls of the mixture in butter until golden brown on both sides. Serve hot with cinnamon and sugar. Serves 4 to 6.

Thin Dutch Pancakes

Flensjes

6 eggs
2 cups milk
1 teaspoon salt

1 cup flour
butter for frying
melted butter
sugar (brown or white)

Beat eggs until frothy; add milk and salt. Pour this mixture into flour, slowly, stirring constantly. In a skillet, melt butter and pour enough batter to coat bottom of skillet. Cook until top is firm and glossy. Turn and cook on the other side. Roll up pancake; cover with the melted butter and sprinkle with sugar. Serve hot. Makes 15 to 20 pancakes.

●●●●●●●●●●●●●●●●●●●●●●●●

Vegetables

Dutch Sites
Sleepy Hollow Restorations
Tarrytown, New York

Beets with Apples

2 large cooked beets
4 tablespoons butter
nutmeg

1 onion, minced
4 tart. apples, chopped
salt
1 tablespoon sugar (optional)

Peel and slice beets. In a saucepan, combine beets, butter, nutmeg, onion, and apples. Season with salt and simmer until reduced to a pulp. Add sugar, if desired. Serves 6.

Brown Beans with Bacon

This is a substantial meal for hungry Dutchmen. Sometimes served with warm syrup, honey, or sorghum.

1 pound dried brown beans
1/2 pound bacon
3/4 pound onions, peeled and chopped

3 medium-sized potatoes, peeled and sliced
1/2 pound leeks, sliced
pepper to taste

Cover the beans with cold water and let soak overnight. Drain and cook in enough water to cover for 1-1/2 to 2 hours or until soft. Drain beans and rinse in cold water. Dice bacon and place in a hot frying pan. When browned, add onion and cook until golden. Add potatoes and leeks and cook until tender. Add the beans; stir and cook until beans have absorbed the bacon drippings. Season to taste. Serves 6.

Cabbage with White Beans

1-1/2 pounds navy beans
1 medium-sized head cabbage,
   coarsely chopped

1 teaspoon salt
5-1/2 tablespoons shortening
6 potatoes, peeled and sliced

Rinse, then cover beans with water and soak overnight. Cook the beans in the same water until almost tender, about 1 hour. Add cabbage and boil for 1/2 hour. Add remaining ingredients and cook for an additional 1/2 hour. Mash and serve. Serves 15.

Cauliflower, the Dutch Way

1 head cauliflower
2 tablespoons butter
2 tablespoons flour

1/2 cup milk
1/2 cup cauliflower cooking liquid
salt and pepper
nutmeg

Remove leaves and bottom of stalk and cook head of cauliflower in boiling salted water until tender, about 20 minutes. Drain, reserving 1/2 cup of the cooking liquid. Melt butter and stir in flour. Gradually add milk and 1/2 cup cauliflower cooking liquid. Heat sauce until thickened. Season to taste. Place cauliflower in a serving dish and pour sauce over. Sprinkle generously with nutmeg.

Dutch Red Cabbage
Rodekool

1 2-pound head red cabbage
2 to 3 tart apples, peeled and sliced
2 to 4 tablespoons butter or margarine

1/4 cup white or brown sugar
1/4 cup vinegar
1/4 teaspoon each allspice, cinnamon, and ground cloves (optional)

Discard core and outer leaves of cabbage and cut rest of cabbage into small pieces. Add apples and cook mixture in boiling salted water until tender, about 30 to 35 minutes. Drain and add butter, sugar, vinegar, and optional spices. Serves 4 to 6.

Endive, Amsterdam Style

Endive is one of the most popular vegetables in Holland.

8 bunches endive, cut into 1/3-inch
    slices
boiling salted water
2 tablespoons butter

2 tablespoons flour
1/2 cup milk
1/2 teaspoon nutmeg
1/2 cup endive stock
salt and pepper

Cook endive in boiling salted water until tender. Drain, reserving the stock. In a saucepan, melt butter and stir in flour. Gradually add milk, nutmeg, and 1/2 cup of the stock to make a medium-thick sauce. Season to taste. Arrange endive on a serving platter and cover with the sauce.

Escarole

Royal Netherlands Embassy, Washington, D.C.

1 head escarole	1 teaspoon butter
2 cups water	2 tablespoons dry bread crumbs
1/2 teaspoon salt	nutmeg

Remove hard outside leaves, then wash and cut the escarole into small pieces. Use the entire head except about 1 inch from bottom. Boil in salted water until tender, about 20 minutes. Drain, add the butter and crumbs, and season to taste with the nutmeg.

Note: A cheese sauce or white sauce over the escarole makes an excellent dish.

Mashed Potato Casserole with Spinach

4 cups mashed potatoes
3 tablespoons butter, divided
1-1/2 to 2 cups milk, divided
2 10-ounce packages frozen, chopped
    spinach, thawed and drained

2 tablespoons flour
pinch of salt
2 ounces American cheese, grated

Combine mashed potatoes with 2 tablespoons butter and 1/2 to 1 cup of milk. Add spinach. In a saucepan, combine 1 cup milk with flour and salt. Stir over low heat until thickened. Add butter and pour over potato mixture. Pour into a greased casserole and sprinkle with cheese. Bake at 350° for 25 to 30 minutes. Serves 8.

Potato-Cheese Soufflé

6 to 8 potatoes, mashed
1/2 cup milk
2 tablespoons butter, melted
2 eggs, separated

salt and pepper
nutmeg to taste
1 cup grated Edam or Gouda cheese

Combine potatoes, milk, butter, egg yolks, salt, pepper, nutmeg, and cheese. Beat egg whites until stiff. Gently fold into potato mixture. Pour into a greased 2-quart casserole and bake at 350° for 25 to 30 minutes or until firm.

Potato Puff

2 tablespoons butter
2 cups mashed potatoes
salt and pepper

2 eggs, separated
3 tablespoons cream

Melt butter in a skillet; add cooked, mashed potatoes, salt, pepper, egg yolks, and cream; stir over low heat until well mixed. Remove from heat. Beat the egg whites until stiff and fold into the potato mixture. Pour into a greased 8x8-inch baking dish and bake at 400° until golden brown, about 12 to 15 minutes. Serves 4.

Potato Rolls

Royal Netherlands Embassy, Washington, D.C.

2 pounds potatoes	3 egg yolks, slightly beaten
4 tablespoons butter, divided	2 tablespoons tomato paste
salt, pepper, and nutmeg	1 cup chopped ham

Peel and cook the potatoes; drain. Purée, adding 2 tablespoons of the butter, then salt, pepper, and nutmeg to taste. Mix in the slightly beaten egg yolks, the tomato paste, and the chopped ham. Heat remaining butter in a skillet. Shape portions (about 1/2 cup) of the potato mixture into oval rolls. Fry in the butter until golden brown on all sides. Makes 12 to 16 rolls.

Mock Hollandaise Sauce

Making a true Hollandaise Sauce can be difficult, so many cooks use this never-fail "mock" version.

1 cup white sauce (recipe next page)　　2 tablespoons butter, melted
2 egg yolks, beaten　　3 tablespoons lemon juice

Pour the cup of white sauce slowly over the beaten egg yolks; blend thoroughly. Add the 2 tablespoons melted butter and when well blended, add the lemon juice. Heat just long enough to cook the egg; stir constantly.

White Sauce for Vegetables

1-1/2 to 2 tablespoons butter or
   margarine
2 tablespoons flour

1/4 teaspoon salt
1 cup milk, divided

Melt butter or margarine in a saucepan. Add the flour and salt all at once and stir until blended. Remove from heat and add 1/3 cup of the milk. Return to heat and continue stirring until mixture begins to thicken, then remove from heat and add another 1/3 cup of the milk; blend until smooth. Add the remaining milk; return to heat and heat to boiling, stirring, slowly. Continue to cook and stir for 1 to 2 minutes.

Main Dishes

Baked Fish

The quantities of this recipe are easily adjustable to size and number of fish.

fish, cleaned and filleted

vinegar

soft bread crumbs

cream

butter, melted

salt

pepper

bacon slices

Wash fish and rub with vinegar inside and out. Moisten the bread crumbs with a little cream and some butter; season to taste with the salt and pepper. Fill fish with the stuffing, then cut slits about 2 inches apart crosswise and place a slice of bacon in each cut. Add some melted butter to a heavy baking dish, then the fish. Baste with the butter, then baste frequently during baking. Bake at 350° until fish is tender and flakes easily.

Baked Mush with Meat
Balkenbrij

Balkenbrij is similar to the scrapple of the Pennsylvania Dutch.

1 pound lean pork	salt
1 pound pork or beef liver	pepper
Water to cover	ground cloves
	buckwheat flour

Place meats in a kettle; add enough water to cover. Season to taste with the salt, pepper, and cloves. Cook until meats are well done and tender; water should be cooked down to about half. Remove the meats and chop or grind until fine. Put ground meat back into the stock and bring mixture back to boiling point; stirring constantly add enough buckwheat flour to make a stiff batter. Spoon batter into loaf pans and chill until firm. To serve, cut thin slices and fry until crisp. **Note:** Good with syrup or molasses for breakfast or a light supper.

Braised Steaks

6 steaks, about 2 to 3 pounds total
salt and pepper
3 tablespoons butter
1-1/2 cups water

1/4 cup vinegar
2 bay leaves
6 peppercorns
1/2 teaspoon cloves
pinch nutmeg

Rub steaks with salt and pepper. Heat the butter
in a saucepan and brown steaks well on both sides.
Add remaining ingredients to pan.
Simmer for 1 to 2 hours, or until steak is very tender.

Croquettes

3 tablespoons butter
3 to 4 tablespoons flour
1 cup milk
1 teaspoon minced parsley
1 to 2 teaspoons minced onion
2 cups minced, cooked chicken

1/2 teaspoon lemon juice
pinch sage
salt and pepper to taste
1 egg
1 tablespoon water
rusk or bread crumbs
oil for frying

In a saucepan, melt butter and stir in flour. Gradually add milk to make a thick sauce. Add parsley, onion, chicken, and lemon juice. Add seasonings. Shape into cones or cylinders. Blend slightly beaten egg and water. Roll cones in crumbs, then in egg mixture, then into crumbs again. Chill. Heat oil to 385° and fry croquettes until golden brown.

Dutch Rarebit

1/4 cup chopped onion
2 tablespoons butter or margarine
1 10-1/2 ounce can condensed
    tomato soup
2 cups grated Edam or Gouda cheese

1 egg, beaten
salt to taste
freshly ground pepper
dash Tabasco
4 to 6 slices white, whole-wheat
    or rye toast

Sauté onion in butter until golden. Add soup and stir well. Add cheese and stir until melted. Add egg and seasonings and cook until thickened. Serve on toast. Serves 4 to 6.

Dutch Spice Roll

5 to 6 pound beef rump roast
   or boned rib roast

3 teaspoons salt
1 teaspoon cloves
1/2 teaspoon pepper

Remove excess fat from meat. Combine spices and rub into meat. Roll meat as for a jellyroll. Tie with string. Wrap a rump roast in foil, but bake a rib roast uncovered. Pour enough water in the bottom of the roasting pan to keep it from becoming dry. Bake at 350° for 2-1/2 to 3 hours. May be sliced for sandwiches when cold.

Note: Nutmeg is often added to spices.

Fillet of Sole with Salmon

1/2 pound salmon, cut into 8 pieces
8 fillets of sole
3 tablespoons butter
3 tablespoons flour
salt and pepper to taste

1-1/2 cups fish stock
1/2 cup white wine
1/2 cup whipping cream
1 egg yolk, beaten
capers and chopped parsley, garnish

Place a piece of salmon at one end of each fillet and roll up and fasten with a toothpick. Cover with salted water and simmer for 6 to 8 minutes or until fish flakes easily. Remove fish and keep warm; remove toothpicks. Melt butter and stir in the flour. Gradually add the seasonings, fish stock, wine, cream, and egg yolk and cook until thickened. Pour over fish and serve garnished with capers and parsley. Serves 8.

Fish Cakes

1/2 cup chopped parsley
3 tablespoons butter
1 pound fish fillets, boiled
1 medium sized onion, chopped

2 eggs
5 rusks, crushed
1/2 cup milk
Salt, pepper, nutmeg, and allspice to taste

Sauté the parsley in butter and combine with the fish. Add remaining ingredients. Mix well, adding additional milk if needed. Shape into round flat cakes and fry until brown on both sides. Serves 4.

Note: Fish Cakes are a good use for leftover fish.

Fruited Barley with Meat

Kruidmoes

2 cups barley
4 quarts water
1 cup dried prunes, soaked
1 cup raisins

1/2 pound salted pork
1/2 cup chopped chervil
1 quart buttermilk
1 ring bologna
1/2 cup corn syrup

Wash barley and cover with water. Cook over low heat for 30 minutes, stirring occasionally. Add prunes, raisins, pork, and chervil. Simmer for 1-1/2 hours, stirring often. Slowly stir in buttermilk; bring to a boil again, stirring constantly. Add bologna and simmer for 10 minutes. Remove pork and bologna, add syrup, and serve with the meat.

Gouda Asparagus Rolls

4 large tomatoes
1 tablespoon bread crumbs
4 ounces Gouda cheese, grated
salt and pepper

4 small sole fillets
8 stalks cooked asparagus
butter
2 cups cooked rice

Cut the tops off the tomatoes and scoop out the centers. Mix the bread crumbs with grated cheese, salt, and pepper. Press the mixture into the tomatoes. Season the fish and roll each around two stalks of asparagus. Stuff each fillet into a tomato. Dot each with butter and place in a baking dish. Bake at 300° for 30 minutes. Serve with rice. Serves 4.

Holland Cheese Chicken Rolls

4 chicken breasts, skinned and boned
1/4 pound Edam or Gouda cheese,
    cut into 8 wedges

flour
2 eggs, beaten
fine dry bread crumbs
oil for deep-frying

Cut each chicken breast in half and pound to about 1/4 inch thickness. Place wedges of cheese on each half and roll, tucking in the edges and securing with a toothpick. Coat the roll with flour, then dip into beaten egg. Roll in bread crumbs and allow to dry for 10 to 15 minutes. Heat oil to 325° and fry rolls for about 10 minutes, or until golden. Serves 4.

Hot Lightning

Hete Bliksem *is a dish that is typical of the Dutch cook's inventive use of available foods. In the middle of the 18th century, when the potato began to replace some of the grain products in the United Provinces, many combinations were tried.*

8 to 10 small potatoes, scrubbed and
    halved
10 slices of bacon, cut into large bits
4 tablespoons butter or margarine,
    melted

salt
pepper
sugar
6 apples or pears, peeled, cored
    and quartered

Put potatoes (cut side down), bacon, and butter or margarine into a casserole; add salt, pepper, and sugar to taste. Bake at 350° for 20 minutes. Add the apples or pears and bake 30 to 40 minutes longer, or until potatoes and fruit are tender.

Note: Slices of sausage may be substituted for the bacon.

Mashed Potatoes with Sauerkraut and Sausage

The Strawtown Inn, Pella, Iowa

6 to 8 large potatoes, halved
butter
1/2 cup milk or cream

1 large jar sauerkraut
1-1/2 pounds smoked sausage,
    cut into 2-inch pieces
nutmeg

Cook potatoes in boiling, salted water until tender. Drain and shake dry. Add butter and milk and mash into a purée. Simmer sauerkraut with sausage about 15 to 20 minutes. Remove sausage and add sauerkraut to potatoes. Mound potato mixture on a large platter and arrange sausage around potatoes. Sprinkle with nutmeg and serve. Serves 6.

Note: Applesauce or glazed apples go well with this dish. *Witloof* (Flemish term meaning chicory, endive) or kale can be used in place of the sauerkraut. Do not use the curly, salad variety of endive.

Meat Loaf Nests

3/4 pound ground veal
3/4 pound ground pork
1/4 teaspoon black pepper
1 teaspoon salt
1/4 teaspoon nutmeg
1/2 cup chopped onion

5 tablespoons butter, melted, divided
1/2 cup soft bread crumbs
1/3 cup milk
6 hard-cooked eggs
1/2 cup dry bread crumbs
1/2 cup water

Combine meats, pepper, salt, and nutmeg. Brown the onion in 2 tablespoons of butter. Combine soft bread crumbs and milk; add to meat mixture with browned onions. Divide into six equal portions. Flatten each portion and place an egg into the center of each; cover egg with meat. Roll meat balls in dry bread crumbs and brown in remaining butter. Add water and simmer for 25 to 30 minutes or until meat is well done. Cut each ball in half and place cut side up on a serving platter. Serves 6.

Netherlands Cheese Pie

4 eggs
2 cups light cream, scalded
1/2 teaspoon salt
freshly ground pepper to taste
pinch nutmeg

pinch cayenne
1 cup shredded Edam or Gouda
cheese
1 9-inch unbaked pie shell

Beat eggs and gradually stir in cream. Stir in seasonings and cheese. Pour into pie shell. Bake at 450° for 12 minutes, then reduce heat to 300° and bake an additional 35 minutes or until set. Serves 6.

Pork Chops with Grapes

salt and freshly ground pepper
4 pork loin chops
Dijon-style mustard

butter
15 to 20 seedless grapes
1/2 cup sour cream

Season pork chops and spread one side with mustard. Heat butter in a skillet and brown the chops mustard side up. Turn and brown the mustard side and spread browned side with mustard. Add grapes to the pan and shake it. Cover and simmer over low heat until chops are tender and cooked through. Remove the chops to a warm platter. Skim most of the fat from the drippings. Add sour cream to pan and heat but do not boil. Pour sauce over meat. Serves 4.

Pork Chops with Chestnuts and Red Cabbage

1/2 small red cabbage, shredded	4 tablespoons butter
16 chestnuts	1 cup chicken stock
4 pork chops	salt and pepper

Soak cabbage in cold water for 1 hour. Shell the chestnuts and cook until soft. (See below.) Fry the pork chops in the butter until browned on both sides. Drain the cabbage and place in a deep casserole. Top with chestnuts and then chops. Add stock and season to taste. Bake covered, at 350° for 1-1/2 hours.

Chestnuts: Cover chestnuts with boiling water and boil them for 15 to 25 minutes; drain and remove the shells and skins. If the meats are not sufficiently tender, cover with boiling water again and cook until tender.

Purée of Potatoes with Ham and Onions

2 pounds potatoes, boiled
1 cup milk
1/2 teaspoon salt

3 tablespoons butter, divided
2 medium-sized onions, chopped fine
1/4 pound ham, diced
3 tablespoons bread crumbs

Mash potatoes and mix in milk and salt. Fry the onion in 2 tablespoons of the butter. In a greased casserole, layer potato mixture, onions, and ham, ending with a layer of potatoes. Sprinkle with bread crumbs and dot with remaining butter. Bake at 350° for 1/2 hour. Serves 6.

Sauerkraut Plate Lunch

1-1/2 pounds sauerkraut
4 thick slices ham, about 1 pound
3/4 cup white wine
3 slices lean bacon

4 frankfurters
4 link sausages, precooked
2 pounds small potatoes,
    peeled and cooked, hot
butter, melted

Spread the sauerkraut in a large heavy pan. Place ham over sauerkraut and pour white wine over all. Cover with bacon. Cook, covered, over low heat for 1 hour. Add frankfurters and sausages; simmer for an additional 20 minutes. Arrange the sauerkraut in a warm flat dish and garnish with the meats and potatoes. Serve with melted butter. Serves 4.

Special Leiden *Hutspot met Klapstuk*
The Strawtown Inn, Pella, Iowa

3 to 4 pounds beef brisket
   or eye of round
2 tablespoons oil
1 to 2 cups beef broth
6 to 8 white potatoes, quartered

6 to 8 carrots, cut in 2-inch pieces
4 large onions, quartered
1/2 rutabaga, finely chopped
1/4 cup butter
1/4 teaspoon white pepper
1/4 teaspoon nutmeg

In a Dutch oven, brown meat in oil. Add broth and cover tightly. Bake at 250° for 3 to 4 hours, or until fork tender. Boil vegetables together in salted water until well done. Drain and shake dry. Mash together, adding butter and seasonings. Slice the meat thin. Mound vegetables on a platter and arrange meat around the vegetables. Pour some of the meat juice over all and serve remaining juice on the side. Serves 6.

Stuffed Veal

6 slices veal
1/4 pound ground veal
1 egg
1 slice white bread
1/4 cup milk

salt, pepper, and nutmeg to taste
4 tablespoons butter
2 lemon slices
1 tablespoon water

Pound the slices of veal until very thin. Mix ground veal with the egg. Soak bread in the milk. Add bread mixture and seasonings to the ground meat mixture. Divide the meat mixture into six portions and place each on a slice of veal. Roll the slices and tie with string. Brown in butter on all sides; add lemon slices and water. Simmer for 45 minutes or until tender. Serves 6.

Note: Can use beef slices in place of veal. A hard-cooked egg or fried onions and parsley can be used in place of meat stuffing.

Traditional *Hotchpotch* with Chuck

On the 3rd of October, many residents of the Netherlands feast on Hutspot met Klapstuk *(rib pieces). Historians say that the dish has been served on that date for 400 years. One theory has it that the tradition began in 1574 when the Dutch fleet drove the Spanish besiegers from Leiden. When the siege was raised on October 3rd, the town's famished citizens and their rescuers supposedly dined on a hastily abandoned kettle of stew simmering over a Spanish campfire.*

2 cups water
1-1/2 teaspoons salt, divided
1-1/2 pounds boneless beef chuck
   or flank steak

6 large carrots, quartered
6 medium-sized potatoes, quartered
6 medium-sized onions, diced
freshly ground black pepper

89

(continued)

Traditional *Hotchpotch* with Chuck   *(continued)*

Bring water and 1 teaspoon salt to a boil. Add meat, cover, and simmer for about 2 hours. Add vegetables and continue cooking for about 1/2 hour or until vegetables are tender. Add more liquid if needed. When this dish is done all the liquid should be absorbed. When tender, remove meat and keep warm; purée the vegetables to a consistency of mashed potatoes, and season with remaining salt and pepper. Place the vegetables in the center of a warm platter and cut meat into thick slices. Arrange around the vegetable purée. Serves 4 to 6.

Flavorful Indonesian Influence

Indonesian food became important in the Netherlands when the East Indies were Dutch Colonies. Many cities and towns have Indonesian and Oriental restaurants. There is the famous *Rijst Tafel* or "Rice Table," which may have as many as twenty to thirty delicacies from main dishes to side accompaniments. The basics include: *Nasi Goreng* (rice) and *Bahmi* (rice or wheat noodles) with meat, poultry, and fish entrées such as Baked Chicken Breasts, Indonesian Shrimp, and Cold Peanut Soup. Side dishes include Chili Seasoning, Coconut Relish, and Baked Bananas. We have included the recipes for this sampling of popular taste. In many homes, *Nasi Goreng* is served weekly, perhaps with an omelet or fried eggs as a contrast with the spiciness. With the *Rijst Tafel* or a *Nasi Goreng* meal, cooled beer is often the beverage of choice.

Note: Indonesian spices and *Nasi Goreng* Mix are available at De Pelikaan, 627 Franklin, Pella, Iowa 50219.

Indonesian Specialties

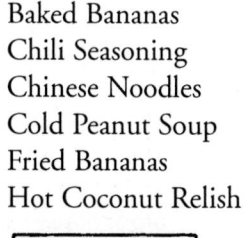

Baked Bananas

4 bananas   pinch of salt
2 tablespoons butter   lemon juice

Peel bananas and cut in half lengthwise. Place in a well-greased baking dish; dot with butter and sprinkle with the salt and lemon juice. Bake at 450° for 6 minutes. Makes 4 servings.

Fried Bananas

4 bananas   1-1/2 tablespoons brown sugar
2 tablespoons butter

Peel bananas and cut in half lengthwise. Arrange in shallow baking dish. Melt butter and stir in brown sugar; pour over bananas. Place in oven under broiler and broil until lightly browned. Makes 4 servings.

Chili Seasoning
Sambal Oelek

Serve with all Indonesian dishes to heighten taste.

2 tablespoons finely chopped red
    chili peppers

1/2 teaspoon salt

1/2 tablespoon oil

1/2 teaspoon lemon juice

1/2 teaspoon grated lemon rind

Mix all ingredients into a paste. Can be kept for some time in a tightly closed jar.

Hot Coconut Relish

1/2 cup coarsely grated coconut

1 small onion, chopped

3 tablespoons lemon juice (or lime)

1 small red hot chili pepper, seeded
and chopped (or 1/4 teaspoon
chili powder)

Combine all ingredients in a blender and blend for 1 minute. Pour into serving dish and let stand 1 hour before serving.

Chinese Noodles
Bahmi

1-1/2 pounds dry Chinese rice noodles
warm water
oil
6 tablespoons shredded leeks
4 tablespoons chopped celery stalks
    and leaves

2 cups shredded Chinese cabbage
2 cloves garlic, minced
2 tablespoons bean sprouts
1/2 pound fried pork, diced
1 cup shrimp or prawns
2 tablespoons soy sauce

Soak noodles in warm water; drain. Add more water and bring to a boil. Turn off heat and soak noodles again until tender, but not too soft; drain. Heat oil and fry leeks, celery, and cabbage with the garlic. Add a little water and bean sprouts and simmer until crisp-tender. Mix vegetables with the noodles; add the meat and shrimp. Season with the soy sauce. Reheat for a few minutes in the oven.

Cold Peanut Soup

4 medium-sized onions, chopped
2 cups beef broth
1 cup milk
1 cup coconut milk (or 1 cup water
   and 1 tablespoon grated coconut)

2 tablespoons peanut butter
dash of paprika
5 tablespoons lime (or lemon) juice
fresh mint (or parsley)
dash of cayenne pepper (optional)

Simmer onions in beef broth for 30 minutes. Strain broth into a bowl. Add the milk, coconut milk, peanut butter, and paprika to the broth. Cover and chill until cold. Stir in lime juice. Serve with garnish of chopped fresh mint or parsley. Cayenne pepper may be added if desired. Serves 4.

Indonesian Baked Chicken Breasts

5 to 6 chicken breasts (2-1/2 pounds)
1/3 cup chunky peanut butter
1/3 cup teriyaki sauce
1/4 cup lemon juice
1/4 cup vegetable oil

1-1/2 teaspoons ground ginger
1-1/2 teaspoons dried sweet basil
2 teaspoons onion powder
1-1/2 teaspoons garlic powder
1/4 teaspoon crushed red pepper

Place chicken breasts in shallow baking dish. Place remaining ingredients in a blender and blend until smooth. Reserve 1/2 cup of sauce; pour remaining sauce over chicken breasts. Turn to coat evenly and marinate in refrigerator for 30 to 40 minutes. Bake at 400° for 45 minutes to 1 hour; baste with the pan sauce 2 or 3 times while baking. Serve with the reserved sauce and rice. Makes 5 to 6 servings.

Indonesian Fried Rice

Nasi Goreng

2 tablespoons vegetable oil
2 medium-sized onions, chopped fine
2 cloves garlic, crushed
1 teaspoon finely chopped red
    chili pepper
1 teaspoon salt

3 cups cooked, cold rice
1/2 pound cooked pork or ham, diced
4 eggs
1 tablespoon water
1 tablespoon butter

In a heavy skillet heat the oil and fry the onions, until browned, with the garlic, red pepper, and salt. Add rice and continue frying until browned; stir frequently with a wooden spoon. Add diced meat and fry 5 minutes more. Beat eggs and water together; heat butter in frying pan and cook egg mixture as an omelette. Cut the omelette into long strips and serve on top of the fried rice. Serves 4. **Note:** This dish is eaten from a soup plate with a spoon and fork. Roasted chicken or shrimp can be used in place of pork or ham.

Indonesian Shrimp

2 large ripe tomatoes, peeled and
    chopped
2 medium-sized onions, sliced
2 red chili peppers, seeded and
    chopped
1 clove garlic, mashed

2 cups coconut milk (or 2 cups water
    and 2 tablespoons grated coconut)
1-1/2 teaspoons sugar
1-1/2 pounds uncooked shrimp,
    peeled and deveined

In a heavy skillet, mix tomatoes, onions, peppers, and garlic. Cook over medium
heat for 5 minutes. Stir constantly. Add coconut milk (or the 2 cups water with
grated coconut), the sugar, and the shrimp. Cook 5 minutes more. Do not
over cook shrimp. Serve over rice. Makes 8 to 10 servings.

Peanut Sauce

A classic Indonesian sauce for burgers, steaks, roast pork, or pork on a skewer.

2-1/2 tablespoons butter or margarine
1 medium-sized onion, finely chopped
1 teaspoon crushed hot red pepper
1 tablespoon soy sauce

4 heaping tablespoons chunky
  peanut butter
1 teaspoon lemon juice
1 cup coconut milk (or 1 cup water
  and 1 tablespoon grated coconut)

Melt butter; add chopped onion and sauté until golden. Add crushed red pepper, soy sauce, and peanut butter. Allow peanut butter to melt, then add lemon juice and coconut milk. Cook and stir until well blended.

Rice

Rijst

This is the Dutch method of cooking plain boiled rice. When properly done, the rice is dry and each grain is separate from the others.

1 cup rice   2 cups cold water

Wash rice in cold water until the water is quite clear, then put rice in a saucepan with twice as much cold water as rice. Cover and bring to a boil quickly. Turn heat down and simmer for 20 minutes. Remove the lid and let stand for 10 minutes till all the moisture has evaporated.

Note: Rice with some butter, white or brown sugar, and cinnamon tossed in is a popular dish.

Cakes, Cookies, and Desserts

Chocolate Nut Cake

1-1/2 cups sugar
3/4 cup butter
3 eggs, separated
1/2 cup cream
2/3 cup cold mashed potatoes
1-1/4 cups flour
2 teaspoons baking powder

3/4 cup bitter chocolate, grated
3/4 cup ground almonds
1/4 teaspoon cloves
1/4 teaspoon nutmeg
1/2 teaspoon cinnamon
1/4 teaspoon salt

Cream sugar and butter. Beat egg yolks. Add yolks and cream, then the potatoes to the creamed mixture. Sift together flour and baking powder. Mix the grated chocolate and ground almonds with the flour, then add the spices and salt. Blend the two mixtures together. Beat the egg whites until stiff and fold into the batter. Pour into two greased 9-inch round cake pans and bake at 375° for 25 to 30 minutes. Frost with any favorite filling or icing.

Dutch Apple Cake

2 cups sifted flour
2 teaspoons baking powder
1/2 teaspoon salt
1/4 cup butter
1 egg
3/4 cup milk

2 cups thinly sliced apples
1/3 cup chopped walnuts
1/3 cup sugar
1 teaspoon cinnamon
1/2 teaspoon nutmeg

Sift together flour, baking powder, and salt. Cut in butter until mixture resembles meal. Beat together egg and milk; quickly stir into flour mixture. Arrange apples and nuts in a 9-inch pie pan. Sprinkle with sugar and spices; spread dough over all. Bake at 350° for 45 minutes. Loosen cake from sides and bottom and invert onto a serving plate while hot. Serves 6.

Note: Good with whipped cream toppings.

Dutch Apple Tart

2 cups flour
3/4 cup butter or margarine, softened
3/4 cup sugar, divided
1 lemon rind, grated

4 apples, peeled and sliced
1/2 cup raisins
1/4 teaspoon cinnamon
2 tablespoons jam of your choice
1 egg, beaten

Combine flour, butter, 1/2 cup sugar, and grated lemon rind. Roll dough out to fit a 9-inch round cake pan, but large enough to trim for top strips. Combine sliced apples, raisins, cinnamon, and jam, and fill the pastry. Roll out dough trimmings and cut strips for top of tart. Brush crust and strips with beaten egg. Bake at 350° for 1 hour.

Dutch Birthday Cake

4 eggs
1-1/4 cups sugar
3/4 cup shortening, softened
1 lemon rind, grated

Filling:
1 cup butter, softened

Frosting:
1-1/2 cups whipping cream
1/2 cup sugar

3 ounces chocolate, melted
2-1/2 cups sifted flour
1/2 teaspoon salt
1 teaspoon baking soda
1 cup milk

3/4 cup powdered sugar
1/4 cup Dutch cocoa

1 teaspoon vanilla
chocolate curls

Beat together eggs, sugar, and shortening until light and fluffy. Blend in lemon rind and chocolate. Sift together flour, salt, and soda. Add flour mixture and milk alternately to creamed mixture. Mix well, then pour into two greased, 9-inch round cake pans. Bake at 350° for 30 minutes or until cake tests done. Cool layers on wire racks.

Filling: Cream butter and sugar. Blend in cocoa. Spread in between cooled cake layers.

Frosting: Beat whipping cream until foamy; add sugar and vanilla. Beat until stiff peaks are formed. Frost cake with mixture and decorate with chocolate curls.

Shortbread

5 cups flour
3 cups sugar
1/2 teaspoon salt
1 teaspoon vanilla

2 cups butter, softened
1 egg
milk
candied cherry halves, slivered
almonds, or preserved ginger

Combine all ingredients except milk and decorations. Knead until the dough is smooth. Press into a 1/2-inch-thick layer on a greased baking sheet. Brush milk over the top and decorate with cherries, almonds, or ginger (arrange pattern for cutting into squares). Bake at 400° for 10 minutes. Turn oven off and leave shortbread in oven for 10 minutes longer. Cut into squares.

Cinnamon Snaps

1 cup sugar
1 cup shortening
1 cup molasses
2 teaspoons baking soda

2 tablespoons warm water
1 tablespoon cinnamon
1 tablespoon ginger
1/2 teaspoon salt
5-1/4 cups flour

Cream sugar and shortening. Add molasses. Dissolve soda in water and add to creamed mixture. Sift together spices, salt, and flour. Add to creamed mixture. These cookies can be rolled out very thin and cut into shapes, or the dough can be placed into a cookie press. Bake on greased baking sheets at 350° for 8 to 10 minutes. Cool on wire rack. Makes 5 dozen.

Dutch Butter Cookies

Martha Lautenbach, Pella, Iowa

Martha is the co-curator of the Scholte House Museum in Pella.

1 cup softened butter
1 cup sugar
2 cups flour

1/4 cup water
1/4 teaspoon baking soda
1 teaspoon vanilla

Cream butter and sugar. Add flour. Combine the water, soda, and vanilla; pour over the first mixture. Stir until the sides of the bowl are clean. Form into a roll and refrigerate until firm. Slice thinly and place on a greased baking sheet. Bake at 350° for 10 to 15 minutes or until golden brown. Makes 3 dozen.

Dutch Handkerchiefs

1 cup butter
2 cups flour
1/4 cup water

1 egg white
1 cup sugar
1 teaspoon almond flavoring

Cut butter into flour. Add water gradually as if making a pie crust. Roll very thin and cut into 4-inch squares. Beat egg white until stiff. Fold in sugar and flavoring. Place about 2 teaspoonfuls of the egg white mixture into the center of each square and fold the corners toward the center of the square. Place on a greased cookie sheet and bake at 350° until lightly browned.

Dutch Pastry Apple Bars

2-1/2 cups flour
1 teaspoon salt
1 cup shortening
1 egg, separated
scant 1/2 cup milk
1 cup corn flakes

8 to 10 apples
1 teaspoon cinnamon
1 cup sugar
1 teaspoon vanilla
1 tablespoon water
1 cup powdered sugar

Mix the flour, salt, shortening, egg yolk, and milk as for a pie crust. Roll half of the dough out to fit a 10x15-inch pan. Sprinkle with corn flakes. Peel and slice apples and place over corn flakes. Sprinkle with cinnamon and sugar. Roll the other half of the dough to cover the apples, sealing the edges. Beat egg white until stiff and brush over dough. Bake at 400° for 1 hour. Combine vanilla, water, and powdered sugar, using more water if needed. Drizzle over warm crust.

Figure Eight Cookies
Krakelingen

1 cup butter
1-1/3 cups sugar
1/4 teaspoon salt
1 teaspoon vanilla
1 egg, beaten, plus milk to
    equal 1/2 cup liquid

2 teaspoons baking powder
4 cups flour
1 egg white
sugar for topping

Cream butter and sugar; add salt, vanilla, and egg mixture. Sift together baking powder and flour. Add to creamed mixture. Mix well and chill. Take small pieces of dough and roll them into the thickness of a pencil. Form figure 8s. Dip into the unbeaten egg white, then the sugar. Place on greased baking sheets and bake at 350° for 10 to 15 minutes. Makes about 5 dozen cookies.

Filled Spice Cookies
"Gevulde" Speculaas

Filling:
1/3 pound almond paste
2/3 cup sugar
Dough:
2/3 cup butter
1/2 cup brown sugar
3/4 teaspoon vanilla
1 egg, beaten
1-3/4 cups flour

1 tablespoon grated lemon peel
1 egg

1-1/2 teaspoons baking powder
1/2 teaspoon salt
1/2 teaspoon cinnamon
1/2 teaspoon nutmeg
1/2 teaspoon allspice
1/2 teaspoon cloves

Filling: Combine ingredients and mix well. **Dough:** Cream butter and sugar; add vanilla and egg. Sift in remaining ingredients and mix well. Divide dough in half and press each into a greased 8x8-inch baking pan. Spread with filling and cover with remaining dough. Bake at 350° for 45 minutes.

Goat Leg Cookies

Bokkepootjes

3 egg whites
1/2 cup sugar
1 cup finely ground almonds
Filling:
1 cup whipping cream
sugar to taste

1 teaspoon cocoa
1 teaspoon instant coffee
Frosting:
1 cup semi-sweet chocolate chips,
  melted

Beat egg whites until stiff, gradually adding the sugar. Fold in the almonds and place in a cookie press. Cover a baking sheet with greased waxed paper. Press almond mixture into ovals on waxed paper. Bake at 250° for 1 hour. Remove paper at once after baking is complete. **Filling:** Beat cream until stiff, adding the remaining ingredients to flavor. Spread over an oval and top with another. Dip both ends in melted chocolate.

115

Johnny Buckshot Cookies

Jan Hagel Koekjes

1-1/2 cups butter
2 cups packed brown sugar
1/8 teaspoon salt
1 egg, beaten

1-3/4 cups flour
1 egg white, slightly beaten
1/2 cup sugar
1/4 teaspoon cinnamon
40 blanched almonds, slivered

Cream butter and sugar; add salt and egg. Sift in flour and mix well. Pat dough into two well-greased jellyroll pans. Brush with beaten egg white. Combine sugar and cinnamon; sprinkle over dough. Sprinkle almonds over dough and press the nuts into the dough. Bake at 350° for 15 to 20 minutes. Cut into squares.

Note: Return pans to oven momentarily if trouble removing cookies from pan.

Lace Cookies
Kletskopjes

1-1/2 cups brown sugar
2 tablespoons water
1/4 cup butter

1 teaspoon cinnamon
1 cup ground almonds
1 cup flour

Make a paste of the sugar and water. Stir in remaining ingredients. Shape dough into 1-inch rounds. Place on a greased baking sheet at least 2 inches apart since they tend to spread or "lace out" when baking. Bake for 15 minutes at 350°. Remove from the oven and let rest for 1/2 minute before removing from baking sheet. Cool on wire rack.

Note: If you have difficulty removing cookies from baking sheet, return the sheet to the oven for a moment.

Small Thumb Cookies

Duimpjes

In the province of Friesland these cookies are served with tea.

1/2 cup butter
3/4 cup sugar
2-1/2 cups flour
1/4 teaspoon salt

2 teaspoons baking powder
1 cup milk
1/2 cup almonds, chopped
1 teaspoon anise seed, chopped

Cream butter and sugar. Sift together flour, salt, and baking powder. Alternately add the dry mixture and the milk to the creamed mixture. Stir in the almonds and anise seed. Place teaspoonfuls onto a greased baking sheet and bake at 400° for 12 minutes or until browned. Makes 4 dozen cookies.

Tongue-Shaped Cookies
Kattetongen

7 tablespoons butter
1/2 cup powdered sugar
1 teaspoon vanilla

salt to taste
2 egg white
3/4 cup flour

Cream butter; add remaining ingredients and mix well. Fill a pastry bag with this dough and use a tube with a straight opening of about 1/2 inch. Make strips about 3 inches long and 1-1/2 inches apart on a greased cookie sheet. Bake at 375° for 5 minutes or until the cookies are brown along the edges but pale in the middle. Remove to racks to cool. Makes 40 to 60 cookies.

Brown Betty or Shoemaker's Tart

9 to 10 apples, peeled, cored and chopped
1-1/4 cups raisins

6 tablespoons butter or margarine
4 eggs, separated
3/4 cup sugar
1 to 1-1/2 cups rusk crumbs

Cook apples until soft. Add raisins and butter or margarine. Beat egg yolks and fold into apple mixture. Beat egg whites until foamy and add sugar; beat until stiff. Fold into apple mixture. Sprinkle 1/2 the rusk crumbs into a greased 9-inch springform pan. Pour 1/3 of apple mixture and sprinkle with 1/3 of the remaining crumbs. Cover with 1/3 of the remaining apple mixture and 1/2 of the remaining crumbs. Layer the last of the apple mixture and the remaining crumbs. Bake at 350° for 50 minutes. Cool and serve with whipped cream or half-and-half.

Cape Clouds

Royal Netherlands Embassy, Washington, D.C.

3 cups milk
vanilla
3 eggs, separated

powdered sugar
2-1/2 tablespoons cornstarch
4 tablespoons sugar

Bring milk and vanilla to a boil; reduce heat but retain slow boil. Beat egg whites until very stiff; beat in some powdered sugar for firmness. With two spoons, form small balls of the egg white; toss the balls in the boiling milk until firm (about 1 minute). Lift out carefully with a skimmer and set aside. Remove milk mixture from heat. Beat together egg yolks, cornstarch, and a small amount of the heated milk mixture (pour heated milk mixture into egg yolks in light stream); stir to warm the egg mixture, then combine the two mixtures. Add the sugar and return to heat. Boil slowly for 3 to 4 minutes until thick. Cool, but stir occasionally to prevent skin forming on top. Pour into a shallow glass dish and top with the egg-white clouds. If desired, sprinkle colored candy-shot on top.

Currant Pudding

1-1/2 envelopes unflavored gelatin
1/4 cup cold water
4 eggs, separated

1/2 cup brown sugar
3/4 cup currant juice
whipped cream

Soften the gelatin in the 1/4 cup cold water. Beat egg yolks and brown sugar until foamy; add the currant juice and heat mixture until thickened. Add the softened gelatin. Stir until gelatin dissolves; remove from heat. Beat egg whites until stiff and fold into the egg yolk mixture. Cool. Stir occasionally until egg whites and custard do not separate, then pour into an oiled pudding mold. Chill and unmold. Serve with sweetened whipped cream.

Dutch Bread Pudding with Almond Sauce

1 14-ounce can sweetened
  condensed milk
3 cups hot water
2 cups day-old bread, crust removed,
  cubed, and packed

3 eggs, beaten
1/4 cup raisins
1/4 cup coconut
1 tablespoon butter, melted
1/2 teaspoon salt
1 teaspoon vanilla

Almond Sauce:
1/2 cup sugar
1 teaspoon cornstarch
1/2 cup water

1/4 cup butter
1 egg, lightly beaten
1 teaspoon almond flavoring

(continued)

Dutch Bread Pudding with Almond Sauce   *(continued)*

Combine milk, water, and bread; cool. Add remaining ingredients and pour into a 2-quart casserole. Place casserole in a pan of water and bake at 350° for 1 hour or until firm. Serve with sauce. Serves 8 to 10.

Almond Sauce: Boil together sugar, cornstarch, water, and butter until sugar is dissolved. Add a little of the hot mixture to the egg and then the egg mixture to the sugar mixture. Cook for 2 to 3 minutes, remove from heat, and add flavoring. Serve warm.

Dutch Prune Dessert

Mina Baker-Roelofs remembers this dessert being served by her mother, Fannie Baker, who received the recipe from her mother. Mina's grandmother, Mrs. Gossen De Boer, came from the Island of Terschelling in the Netherlands.

3 slices bread	water
1 cup milk	butter
30 prunes, pitted	brown sugar

Soak bread in milk until soaked through. Cook prunes in water to cover until soft; drain and reserve juice. Place prunes and 1-1/2 cups of the juice in a heavy saucepan and add the bread mixture. Cook over low heat for 1 hour. Do not stir but keep the prunes free from the bottom of the pan with a fork. Over stirring will cause the dessert to become pasty. Add additional milk if necessary. Serve hot with butter and brown sugar. Serves 6.

Heavenly Mud

Annie Veldhuis, Des Moines, Iowa
Annie was formerly of Epe, Gelderland Holland. Puddings are very popular for dessert.

3 cups milk, divided
2 eggs, separated
3 tablespoons sugar
3 tablespoons cornstarch

1 teaspoon vanilla
1/2 cup raspberry or
    strawberry preserves

Bring 2-1/2 cups of the milk to a boil over medium heat. Beat egg yolks till foamy; add sugar mixed with cornstarch, 1/2 cup cold milk, and vanilla. Stir until smooth, then gradually stir in the hot milk. Heat mixture to a boil, stirring constantly. Boil for 2 minutes; cool thoroughly. Beat egg whites until stiff; continue beating while slowly adding preserves. Pile the beaten egg white mixture by spoonfuls on top of cooled pudding. Serves 6.

John in the Sack

Jan in De Zak

This odd name derives from the fact that it used to be made with a clean white pillow case instead of a mold.

1 package active dry yeast
1/4 cup lukewarm water
3 cups sifted flour
3/4 cup milk, scalded and
    cooled to lukewarm

1 egg
1/3 cup currants
1/3 cup raisins
salt

Dissolve yeast in water. Combine flour, milk, and egg; mix well. Add fruit and salt, then the yeast mixture, and blend. Cover and let rise for 45 minutes. Fill a steamed pudding mold 2/3 full with dough; cover and steam for 2 to 3 hours or until done. Serve hot with molasses sauce or melted butter and brown sugar.
Note: A taut string can be used to cut slices of the warm pudding.

Lemon Chiffon Cream

4 eggs, separated
1/2 cup sugar
rind of 1 lemon, grated

juice of 2 lemons
1/2 cup dry white wine
6 to 8 lemon slices
small cookies or wafers

Beat egg yolks and sugar until white and fluffy. Add lemon rind and gradually stir in lemon juice and wine. Pour into the top of a double boiler and heat, but do not boil; stir vigorously until mixture stiffens. Set aside to cool. Beat egg whites until stiff and fold into slightly cooled cream mixture. Chill and serve garnished with lemon slices and small cookies or wafers. Serves 6 to 8.

Limburg Tart

Limburgse Vlaaien

Limburgse Vlaaien *is a type of tart or pie most popular in the Southern Province of Limburg, Holland, where the famous pottery city of Maastricht is located. Almost like American pie, this tart has a thicker bottom crust and is made with a sweet, rich bread dough.*

2-1/4 cups flour
1/4 cup sugar
1 teaspoon salt
1 1-ounce cake yeast
1/4 cup butter
1 egg

1/4 cup milk, lukewarm
2 pounds sliced peaches or apricots, plums, or other fruit, sweetened and stewed
additional sugar for sprinkling

(continued)

Limburg Tart   *(continued)*

Mix flour, 1/4 cup sugar, and 1 teaspoon salt in a large bowl. Stir yeast, butter, and egg into milk. Stir into flour mixture. Knead, cover, and let rise until doubled, about 1 hour. Roll 3/4 of the dough to fit lightly greased 10-inch pie tin; allow to rise again until doubled. Prick with a fork to release air bubbles, then fill with the stewed fruit. Roll out remaining dough and cut into strips. Lay the strips crisscross over the fruit. Bake at 450° for 25 to 30 minutes. Sprinkle with additional sugar immediately after removing from the oven.

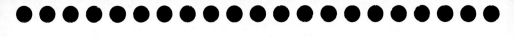

Rhubarb Casserole

2 pounds rhubarb
sugar to taste

1-1/2 cup rusk crumbs, divided
cinnamon to taste
2 tablespoons butter, melted

Cut rhubarb into 1-inch pieces and cook in a little water until well-done. Stir until mixture resembles applesauce and add sugar to taste. Mix 1/4 cup rusk crumbs, sugar, and cinnamon to taste. Set aside. Combine remaining crumbs with the butter and press into an 8x8-inch baking pan. Pour rhubarb over crumbs and sprinkle with the remaining crumb mixture. Bake at 350° until browned, about 15 to 20 minutes.

Zuider Zee Pudding

Crust:

1 5-ounce package rusk, crushed, or
    2-1/2 cups graham cracker crumbs

1/2 cup butter, melted
1/4 to 1/2 cup sugar

Filling:

3/4 cup sugar
6 tablespoons cornstarch
1/2 teaspoon salt

3-1/2 cups milk, scalded
4 egg yolks
1 teaspoon vanilla

Meringue:

4 egg whites
3/4 teaspoon cream of tartar

1/2 cup sugar
1/4 cup chopped walnuts or almonds

Crust: Combine all ingredients and set aside 1/4 of the mixture. Use the remaining mixture to line a 9-inch springform pan or an 8x8-inch baking pan. Press crumbs in firmly.

Filling: Combine sugar, cornstarch, and salt; gradually add milk, stirring constantly. Cook in the top of a double boiler for 18 minutes, stirring constantly until thickened. Beat egg yolks slightly and pour part of the hot mixture over them, mixing well. Return mixture to the double boiler. Cook about 2 minutes longer, stirring constantly. Remove from heat; add vanilla. Cool and pour into crumb-lined pan.

Meringue: Beat egg whites until foamy; sprinkle cream of tartar over whites and beat until stiff. Beat in sugar gradually. Spread over filling and sprinkle with the nuts and reserved crumb mixture. Bake at 325° about 15 minutes or until delicately browned. Serve cold. Serves 8 to 9.

Christmas Holiday Traditions

Holidays bring Dutch treats. The official beginning of the Dutch Christmas season is December 6, Sinterklaas Day. Sinterklaas was originally a stately bishop, dressed in a bright red cape and mitre, who arrived in Holland by boat from Spain. Each December 5, St. Nicholas Eve, Dutch children set out wooden shoes with hay or a carrot for Sinterklaas's horse. The next morning, good boys and girls find a sweet treat, but bad children find a piece of coal.

Large Speculaas (spice cookies or cakes), "gingerbread people," are typical treats delivered by Sinterklaas. There was a custom in the olden days for him to deliver a Speculaas in the form of a man to the spinsters, while the bachelors received a woman-shaped cake. The treats are often personalized, such as the Dutch Letters made in the shape of the initial letter of the recipient's name, or "M" for mothers. The Speculaas Cookie and Dutch Letter recipes are included in the following collection of traditional Dutch Christmas treats.

A Traditional Christmas Dinner Menu

Traditionally favorite foods will usually be found at family dining tables on holidays. The following menu prepared by the Strawtown Inn restaurant in Pella, Iowa, reflects a traditionally bountiful, delicious Dutch Christmas dinner.

VOOGERECHTEN
Bitterballe Met Hollandse Mostard
(Little Meatballs with Dutch Mustard)

Kaasbolletjes
(Little Cheeseballs)

VIS
Schol met Mostard Saus
(Haddock with Mustard Sauce)

ENTREE
Blinde Vinken met Champignon Saus
(Stuffed Fillet of Veal with Mushroom Sauce)
Stamp Pot van Aardappelen en Groeten
(Whipped Potatoes with Greens)
Rode Kool
(Red Cabbage)

SLA
Komkommer en Tomaten Vinaigrette
(Cucumber and Tomatoes)

SOEP
Heldere Ossentaart
(Clear Oxtail Soup with Vegetables)

NAGERECHT
Chocolat ljs met Banket
(Dutch Chocolate Ice Cream with Almond Pastry)
Snoeps van Sint Nicholas
(Treats from St. Nick)
Koffie - Thee
(Coffee and Tea)

Holiday Treats

Dutch Crullers

In the Netherlands, Poffertjes, *small, light, fluffy crullers, are for special occasions. Iron molds are often used. This recipe suggests making the crullers without the mold.*

4 tablespoons sugar	1 teaspoon grated orange rind
1 teaspoon salt	1 cup flour
4 tablespoons fat	3 eggs
1 cup hot water	fat or oil for deep-frying
	powdered sugar

Put sugar, salt, fat, water, and orange rind into a saucepan. Heat to boiling point; add flour and mix well. Cook until thickened; stir constantly. Cool slightly. Add one egg at a time, beat thoroughly after each addition. Press dough through a pastry bag, one cruller at a time, onto a well-greased square of heavy paper. Turn paper over and let cruller drop into the hot fat. Fry 6 to 7 minutes until well puffed and a delicate brown. Drain, then drizzle with powdered sugar.

Dutch Fondant

Borstplaat

From Nella Kennedy, archivist and instructor of Dutch history and language at Northwestern College, Orange City, Iowa

4 tablespoons butter	12 drops green food coloring
6 to 7 cups sifted powdered sugar	1/2 teaspoon peppermint extract
3 tablespoons evaporated milk	

Combine butter and 2 cups of the powdered sugar; stir in milk. Mix in 3 to 4 more cups of sugar. Turn onto a sugared surface and knead in more sugar until moderately stiff. Divide mixture in half and cover. Make a well in one half; add coloring and peppermint; knead until color is even. Divide green and white mixtures into fourths and shape each into a 5-inch square. Cover when shaped. Place green square atop white; roll up, jellyroll fashion. Seal side seam and roll carefully on lightly sugared surface to 1 to 2-1/2 inch diameter. Wrap in foil; chill. Repeat process to make four rolls. Slice into 1/2-inch pieces; wrap and refrigerate.

Dutch Letters
Dutch Banket

Dottie DeVries, Pella, Iowa, uses this pie crust method for making Dutch Letters.

Dough:
1 pound butter or margarine
4 cups flour
1 cup water
2 egg whites, slightly beaten

Filling:
1 pound almond paste
2 cups sugar
3 eggs
1 teaspoon vanilla

Dough: Mix butter and flour. Stir in water and mix to form dough. Chill overnight or longer.

Filling: Beat almond paste until smooth; add sugar, eggs, and vanilla; mix well and chill.

(continued)

Dutch Letters   *(continued)*

Assembly: When ready to bake, divide dough and filling into fourteen equal parts. Roll one section of dough into a 14x4-1/2-inch strip, then take a tablespoon of filling and spread it down the center of the dough strip. Lap one side of dough over the filling, then the other side, and pinch ends shut. Shape letter; place on greased cookie sheet with seam on bottom.

Brush tops with beaten egg whites
and sprinkle sugar on top;
prick with a fork every 2 inches
to allow steam to escape.
Bake at 400° for 30 minutes.
Makes 14 letters.

140

Jaarsma's Dutch Letters

Visitors to Pella, Iowa, can hardly come away without a bag of Dutch letters.
Ralph Jaarsma of Jaarsma's Bakery gives this puff pastry method recipe.

4-1/2 cups all-purpose flour	1 can (8 ounces) almond paste
1 teaspoon salt	1 cup sugar, divided
1 pound butter	1/2 cup brown sugar
1 egg	2 egg whites
1 cup water	milk

In a large mixing bowl, combine flour and salt. Cut butter into 1/2-inch slices. Stir into flour mixture, coating each piece to separate it. (Butter will be in large chunks.) In a small bowl, combine egg and water. Add all at once to the flour mixture. Mix quickly. (Butter will still be in 1/2-inch pieces, and flour will not be completely moistened.)

(continued)

Jaarsma's Dutch Letters *(continued)*

Turn the dough onto a lightly floured surface and knead it ten times, pressing and pushing dough pieces together to form a rough-looking ball. Shape the dough into a rectangle. (Dough still will have some dry-looking areas.) Flatten the dough slightly. Working on a well-floured surface, roll out the dough to a 15x10-inch rectangle. Fold the two short sides to meet in center and then fold in half to form four layers (this should give you a 5x7-1/2-inch rectangle). Repeat the rolling and folding process once.

Cover the dough with plastic wrap; chill it for 20 minutes. Repeat rolling and folding two more times and chill 20 minutes more. Meanwhile, in a small mixing bowl, combine the almond paste, 1/2 cup of the sugar, brown sugar, and egg whites; beat until the mixture is smooth; set aside.

Cut chilled dough crosswise into four equal parts. Keep unused dough chilled. Roll part of the dough into a 12-1/2x10-inch rectangle. Cut into five 10x2-1/2-inch strips. Spread 1 slightly rounded tablespoon of the almond mixture down center third of each strip. Roll up each strip lengthwise. Brush edge and ends with milk or water. Pinch to seal. Place seam-side down on ungreased baking sheet, shaping each into the letter "S" or desired letter. Brush with milk and sprinkle with sugar. Repeat with remaining dough and filling. Bake in a 375° oven for 25 to 30 minutes or until golden. Cool on wire racks. Makes 20.

Old Ladies' Cake for Christmas

Oude Dame Koek

2 tablespoons butter
1 cup sugar
1 egg, beaten
1/2 cup molasses
1/2 cup honey
1-1/2 teaspoons ground anise seed
2 cups sifted cake flour

1 teaspoon baking powder
1 teaspoon baking soda
1/2 teaspoon salt
1/2 teaspoon nutmeg
1/2 teaspoon allspice
1/2 teaspoon cloves
1-1/2 cups buttermilk

Cream butter and sugar; add egg, molasses, honey, and anise. Beat well. Sift together flour, baking powder, soda, salt, and spices. Alternately add dry mixture and buttermilk to butter mixture. Pour batter into a greased 9-inch tube pan. Bake at 300° for 45 minutes.

St. Nicholas Icebox Cookies

1 cup sugar
1 cup brown sugar
1 cup margarine
1 cup butter
3 eggs, beaten

3-1/2 cups flour
1 teaspoon baking soda
2 teaspoons cinnamon
1/2 teaspoon nutmeg
1 cup finely chopped nuts

Cream sugars, margarine, and butter; add eggs. Sift together flour, soda, and spices. Add to creamed mixture. Mix in the nuts. Divide dough and shape into rolls, 2 inches in diameter. Cover and refrigerate overnight. Slice rolls thinly and place slices on greased baking sheets. Bake at 350° for 12 minutes or until golden brown.

Spice Cookies

Speculaas Koekjes

This recipe is an old favorite from Jaarsma's Bakery in Pella, Iowa. Traditionally, this dough is used to form "gingerbread people" in wooden cookie molds.

1-1/2 cups butter	1 teaspoon cinnamon
2 cups brown sugar	3/4 teaspoon ground cloves
3-1/2 cups flour	1/2 teaspoon nutmeg
1 egg, beaten	1/2 teaspoon allspice
1 teaspoon baking powder	1/2 teaspoon ground ginger
1 scant teaspoon salt	

Cream butter and sugar; add remaining ingredients and stir to form a very stiff dough. Shape dough into a cylinder the diameter equal to the desired cookie size; cover and chill thoroughly. Slice chilled dough; place on lightly greased cookie sheet and bake at 350° for 10 to 12 minutes. Store in tightly covered container. **Variation:** Press well-chilled dough into molded cookie boards.

Dutch Doughnuts or Dumplings with Baking Powder

These doughnuts, Oliebollen, *are a traditional treat on New Year's Eve in Holland and are seldom or never eaten on any other day of the year. Dutch children delight in eating* Oliebollen *until midnight, or being awakened to eat this Dutch treat at the stroke of the New Year.*

2 cups flour
1/4 cup sugar
3 teaspoons baking powder
1 teaspoon salt
1 teaspoon nutmeg

1/4 cup vegetable oil
3/4 cup milk
1 egg
citron or raisins (optional)
fat or oil for frying
powdered sugar

Sift together dry ingredients; stir in remaining ingredients with a fork. Mix thoroughly. Drop batter by teaspoonfuls into hot, 375°, fat or oil; fry till golden brown. Drain on absorbent paper; roll warm puffs in powdered sugar. Makes 30.

Dutch Fritters or Doughnuts with Yeast

2 cakes compressed yeast
2 cups lukewarm water or milk
1/2 cup sugar
2 eggs, slightly beaten
1/2 cup shortening, softened
7 to 7-1/2 cups sifted flour

2 teaspoons salt
4 cups chopped uncooked apples
1-1/4 cups raisins
1 cup currants
oil for deep-frying
powdered sugar

Blend yeast with the lukewarm water or milk; stir in sugar, eggs, and softened shortening. Sift together flour and salt; add the yeast mixture and mix until blended. Stir in apples, raisins, and currants. Let batter rise in a warm place until doubled. Break off by spoonfuls and deep-fry in hot oil, 375°, until golden brown. Drain on absorbent paper and roll in powdered sugar. Mix cinnamon with powdered sugar if desired. Makes 6 to 7 dozen.

Snowballs

Sneeuwballen

This puff pastry is frequently served on New Year's Eve.

1/2 cup cold water
1/4 teaspoon salt
1/2 cup margarine
1/2 cup plus 2 tablespoons flour
3 eggs

3 tablespoons raisins
2 tablespoons finally cut citron or
    dried fruit mix
1 teaspoon vanilla
fat or oil for deep-frying

Place water, salt, and margarine in a saucepan; bring to a boil. Remove from heat and add the flour. Stir until smooth. Beat in eggs one at a time; beat well. Mix in fruit and vanilla. Heat fat or oil to 360° to 375°. Drop balls of the dough into the fat and fry till golden brown. Drain on absorbent paper, then roll warm balls in powdered sugar. Makes 2 dozen.

A Dutch-American "Coffee Table"

An authentic Dutch *Koffie Tafel,* "Coffee Table," is an easy way to entertain at Christmastime. The foods should be readily available, easily prepared, and convenient to serve. Typically the "Coffee Table" might include:

Dried Beef Rolls

Cold Cuts *(sliced ham, bologna)*

Assorted Cheeses *(Edam and Gouda cheese with red rinds)*

Pigs in the Blanket

Assorted Breads and Rolls *(bakery select)*

Butter, Jam *(other condiments)*

Assorted Fruits *(apples, bananas, oranges, etc.)*

Dutch Hot Chocolate, Dutch Coffee

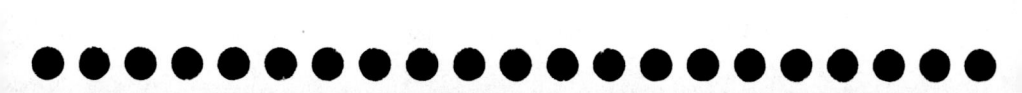

Pigs in the Blanket
Saucijzebroodjes

Dough:
2 cups flour
1/2 teaspoon salt
2 teaspoons baking powder
1/2 cup vegetable shortening
1 egg, beaten
1/2 cup milk (approximately)

Filling:
1 pound lean pork sausage
1/2 pound ground beef
2 Dutch rusks, crushed, or 1/4 cup
    bread crumbs
2 tablespoons cream
salt and pepper to taste

Dough: Sift dry ingredients together. Cut shortening into flour mixture. Mix beaten egg and milk (total 3/4 cup liquid); add to first mixture. On floured surface, blend and knead 8 to 10 times. Divide dough into two parts and roll each half to 1/4 inch thickness. Use a medium-sized cookie cutter to cut fifteen rounds of dough from each half.

(continued)

Pigs in the Blanket   *(continued)*

Filling: Blend all ingredients together. Shape thirty small rolls of meat (like link sausages).

Assembly: Place one roll of filling in each pastry round; fold pastry over the filling and seal edges. Place on baking sheets with raised edges. Bake at 350° for 40 minutes. Baking temperature and time are important in order to cook the meat thoroughly. Serve hot. Makes 30 Pigs.

Note: If convenient, these can be made ahead of time; refrigerate or freeze and reheat before serving. They are a special treat at the "Coffee Table."

Sites and Events Celebrating Dutch Heritage

This listing is just a sampling of Dutch sites and events, but represents the contributions made by Dutch Americans across the nation.

California

Golden Gate Park, San Francisco. The Old Dutch Mill (85 feet high) and the Murphy windmill (95 feet high) pump water to the three lakes in the park.

In **Solvang** there is a blue-trimmed Dutch store graced by a windmill.

Colorado

Denver's Bethesda Hospital's Dutch Festival, held in June each year, includes a parade of costumes, wooden shoe carving, klompen dancing, displays of Dutch arts and crafts, and other events of Dutch culture.

Delaware

Winterthur Museum displays rare artifacts of Dutch heritage.

Illinois

Fulton's Tulip Festival in May is a vibrant celebration of Dutch culture.

Iowa

Orange City, settled by Dutch pioneers, has a charming windmill with furnishings imported from Holland and a Delft tile fireplace. The annual Tulip Festival is a celebration of tradition that attracts thousands of visitors.

Pella is a picturesque small city with architectural influences remindful of the Netherlands. A strong Dutch heritage preserves the culture in its restaurants, events, and sites. The annual Tulip Festival held each May finds residents in Dutch costume; streets and gardens ablaze with tulips; special events in the Historic Village (a complex of buildings portraying early Dutch life);

klompen dancing; street scrubbing; parades; pageants; and exhibits. Year-round, visitors tour the Village and the historic Scholte House Museum, see the *klokken-spel* on the town square; and enjoy traditional Dutch dining. The Christmas season is also a special time for celebrating. The arrival of *Sinterklaas* on the day after Thanksgiving opens this festive season. The decorated Historic Village, shops, the *klokkenspel's* merry Christmas figures, a magnificent tree of Dutch Heritage lace in the Scholte House, home tours, and other events welcome thousands of visitors.

Michigan

In **Grand Rapids** many Dutch artifacts depicting the area's Dutch heritage are found in the Gerald R. Ford Museum.

Holland is a major site of Dutch America with the Netherlands Museum, wooden shoe factories, and the spectacular Windmill Island. Here visitors can see the multi-story De Zwaan windmill, old Dutch carousel, Dutch architecture and gardens, and the popular Dutch Theme Park. During the annual Tulip Festival, special events celebrate Dutch-American culture.

In **Zeeland** a walking tour includes architectural examples and historic homes built by Dutch immigrants. The Museum houses a display of dolls in traditional costumes of all the Netherland provinces.

Minnesota

Edgerton holds an annual Dutch Days celebration in July.

New York

Albany, the capital city, holds a Tulip Festival, a *Kinderkemis* (children's fair), and a *Pinksterfest* (Whitsuntide or fifty days after Easter) in the spring when celebrating abounds. At the University Plaza, see the nation's largest weather vane, a two-ton copper replica of the *Halve Maen* (Half Moon), Henry Hudson's ship that sailed up the famous river. Other historic sites include: First Church

(Reformed) with a pulpit carved in Holland; the 1787 Georgian frame house, Cherry Hill, home of the pioneer Van Rensselaer family; Schuyler Mansion, a 1761 brick Georgian house built by Revolutionary War General Philip Schuyler (Alexander Hamilton's father-in-law); and the Ten Broeck Mansion, 1798 brick Federal style. The New York State Library and the Albany Institute of History and Art contain treasures of Dutch heritage.

Coxsackie has the Bronck House Museum (circa 1663), which displays 18th- and 19th-century Dutch furnishings.

Fishkill's Van Wyck Homestead Museum houses Dutch artifacts. Its old Dutch Reformed Church, used as a prison during the Revolutionary War, has been preserved and is open to the public.

At **Hurley,** on the second Saturday of July, a tour of historic houses is sponsored by the Dutch Reformed Church.

Kinderhook's Luykas Van Alen House is a restoration museum of Dutch architectural style, featuring the Ichabod Crane School House Museum, named for the teacher in *The Legend of Sleepy Hollow;* an Antique Festival is held in June. During the Christmas season an annual decorative greens show is held at the James Vanderpoel "House of History," where there is also an architectural-elements show in May and a farm show in August. Lindenwald, the home of former president Martin Van Buren, is open to the public.

In **Kingston,** once the capital city of New York, is the Abraham Van Gaasbeck House, now called the Senate House, which is open at appointed hours.

In **New York City,** The City of New York Museum contains artifacts and crafts of the Dutch who founded the city.

At **Rensselaer,** the Crailo State Historic Site includes many examples of Dutch-Colonial life.

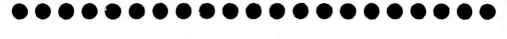

Schenectady features preservation of Dutch-Colonial architecture. The restored Abraham Yates House (circa 1700) is open to the public.

On **Staten Island,** the Richmondtown Restorations feature buildings erected by early Dutch settlers and the Voorlezer's House (circa 1696).

Tarrytown's Historic Hudson Valley is a network of 6 historic sites in Sleepy Hollow country, including: Sunnyside, home of author Washington Irving, creator of the legendary Rip Van Winkle; Kykuit, the Rockefeller estate; Van Cortlandt Manor; and Philipsburg Manor. All are open to the public.

Oregon

Woodburn has a spring tulip festival hosted by the Wooden Shoe Bulb Company, just east of the town.

Washington

Oak Harbor celebrates a Holland Happening in April.

Woodland has a spring festival for three weeks in April, hosted by the Holland America Bulb Farms.

Wisconsin

Cedar Grove holds a Holland Festival in July.

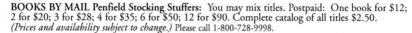

BOOKS BY MAIL Penfield Stocking Stuffers: You may mix titles. Postpaid: One book for $12; 2 for $20; 3 for $28; 4 for $35; 6 for $50; 12 for $90. Complete catalog of all titles $2.50. *(Prices and availability subject to change.)* Please call 1-800-728-9998.

Æbleskiver and More (Danish)
Dandy Dutch Recipes
Dutch Style Recipes
Dear Danish Recipes
Fine Finnish Foods
French Recipes
German Style Recipes
Great German Recipes
Norwegian Recipes
Norwegian Centennial
Scandinavian Holiday Recipes
Scandinavian Smorgasbord Recipes
Scandinavian Style Fish and Seafood Recipes
Scandinavian Sweet Treats
Splendid Swedish Recipes
Time-Honored Norwegian Recipes
Waffles, Flapjacks, Pancakes
Slavic Specialties

Pleasing Polish Recipes
Cherished Czech Recipes
Czech & Slovak Kolaches & Sweet Treats
Quality Czech Mushroom Recipes
Quality Dumpling Recipes
Amish Mennonite Recipes & Traditions
American Gothic Cookbook
Recipes from Ireland
Recipes from Old Mexico
Savory Scottish Recipes
Ukrainian Recipes
Tales from Texas Tables
Texas Cookoff
License to Cook Series:
Italian Style; Texas Style; Alaska Style;
Arizona Style; Iowa Style; Minnesota Style;
New Mexico Style; Oregon Style;
Wisconsin Style; Missouri Style

PENFIELD BOOKS • 215 BROWN STREET • IOWA CITY, IA 52245-5801 • WWW.PENFIELDBOOKS.COM

ls de buik zat is, is 't harte vro lijk.

When the stomach is full,
the heart is glad.

Dutch Proverb

● ●